AF255463

The Anatomy of Human Being

The Anatomy of Human Being

By

CONDE CAGALITAN

Dedication

For those who hunger for Truth.

Published by Conde Cagalitan

ISBN: 978-1-7645121-8-3

Printed in the United States of America

Table of contents

Preface

This book is an anatomy — a structural exploration of
the human condition.

It is not a system, a doctrine, or a philosophy.

It is a map of the heart, the self, the ego, the mind, and
the world.

It is the story of how the architecture of Being was lost,

and how it can be restored.

You will not find arguments here.

You will find a mirror.

If something in these pages awakens you,

follow it.

The movements that follow are not instructions.

They are revelations.

Introduction

Every human being lives from an architecture they cannot see.

This book reveals that architecture.

It begins with the foundation of Being,

descends into the inward turn,

passes through agony and impossibility,

and arrives at the moment when Truth enters the heart.

From there, the architecture turns outward again —

toward restoration, vocation, and alignment.

This is the story of every human being.

This is the story of Being itself.

MOVEMENT I

The Ground We Stand On
How Every Discipline Tries to Explain Man
Why None Can Reach the Heart

Every discipline that attempts to explain the human
being begins with a foundation.
A starting point.
A premise about what man is.

But none of these foundations begin where man
actually began.
None begin in the Garden.
None begin with the Source.
None begin with the heart.

Because they begin in the wrong place, they can only
ever explain fragments of man.
Pieces.
Behaviours.
Patterns.
Symptoms.

Never the architecture.
Never the origin.
Never the hidden heart.

This is why the world has thousands of explanations of
man, yet no coherent understanding of being.

Philosophy

Philosophy begins with the mind.
It assumes that man is fundamentally a thinking
creature.
It builds its explanations on reason, logic,
consciousness, identity.

But the mind is not the source of man.
The mind is not the actor.
The mind is not the origin of motive or drift.

The mind is only the projection screen of the self.

Philosophy begins too late.

Psychology

Psychology begins with behaviour.
It assumes that man is fundamentally a behaving
creature.
It studies patterns, trauma, coping, cognition.

But behaviour is the fruit, not the root.
It is the expression, not the cause.

Psychology begins too shallow.

Neuroscience

Neuroscience begins with the brain.
It assumes that man is fundamentally a biological
creature.
It measures activity, chemicals, circuits, impulses.

But the brain is hardware.
It cannot reveal motive.
It cannot reveal the self.
It cannot reveal the heart.

Neuroscience begins too low.

Sociology

Sociology begins with society.
It assumes that man is fundamentally a social creature.
It studies systems, groups, structures, institutions.

But society is the mirror of man, not the maker of man.
It reflects the heart; it does not explain it.

Sociology begins too wide.

Anthropology

Anthropology begins with culture.
It assumes that man is fundamentally a cultural
creature.
It studies rituals, customs, evolution, development.

But culture is the expression of the heart, not its origin.
It is the outward pattern of an inward condition.

Anthropology begins too late.

Evolution

Evolution begins with survival.
It assumes that man is fundamentally a biological
organism shaped by adaptation.
It explains physical development, traits, and
mechanisms.

But evolution cannot explain the self.
It cannot explain the ego.
It cannot explain fantasy.
It cannot explain the hidden heart.
It cannot explain the turning in the Garden.

Evolution describes the body, not the being.

Evolution begins too far from the center.

Science

Science begins with the measurable.
It assumes that man is fundamentally a physical system.
It studies what can be observed, repeated, quantified.

But the heart is not measurable.
The self is not observable.
The ego is not quantifiable.
Fantasy is not repeatable.
Motive cannot be placed under a microscope.

Science explains the mechanism, not the meaning.
It explains the process, not the purpose.

Science begins outside the interior.

Theology

Traditional theology begins with doctrine.
It assumes that man is fundamentally a moral creature.
It names sin, rebellion, fallenness, redemption.

But it rarely diagrams the mechanism of the heart.
It reveals the truth, but not the architecture.
It names the condition, but not the structure.

Theology begins with the answer, not the anatomy.

The Result

Every discipline explains something.
None explain being.

They describe the branches.
None reveal the root.

They interpret the fruit.
None expose the tree.

They analyze the symptoms.
None uncover the source.

They begin everywhere except where man began.

MOVEMENT II

The Architecture of The Being
The Design of Man Before the Turning

To understand the human condition, we must first understand the human design.
Before the fall, before the turning, before the heart hid itself, the Being existed in a state that no modern discipline can imagine and no scientific model can reconstruct.

Genesis 2 is the only record of the human Being in its original architecture.
It is the only place where the structure of man is revealed without distortion.

This movement reconstructs that architecture through inference, Scripture, and the visible consequences of what was lost.

The Being Was Formed, Not Emerged

The human Being did not arise from accident, adaptation, or evolutionary drift.
It was formed intentionally.

Formation implies:

- purpose

- structure

- design

- alignment

- coherence

The Being begins as a created entity, not a self-constructed one.

This is the first pillar of the anatomy.

The Being Was Breathed Into

The breath given to the Being is not biological
animation.
It is identity.
It is meaning.
It is the interior life of the heart.

This breath establishes:

- the heart as the center

- the self as relational

- the mind as servant

- the world as context

- the Source as origin

The Being is not self-generated.
It is received.

The Being Was Placed

Placement is not geography.
It is environment, order, and alignment.

The Garden is the environment of:

- openness

- transparency

- relational identity

- external truth

- given meaning

- received purpose

The Being is not autonomous.
It is situated.

The Being Was Called

The Being is given responsibility and participation.
Naming is not classification; it is co-creation.
It is the exercise of authority under alignment.

This calling reveals:

- the heart as responsive

- the self as outward-facing

- the ego as dormant

- the mind as interpreter

- the world as partner

The Being is not passive.
It is active within order.

The Being Was Warned

The boundary given in the Garden is not a restriction.
It is a structural truth.

If the Being turns inward, it collapses.
If the heart becomes its own source, it dies.
If the self becomes central, the architecture breaks.

The warning reveals:

- the heart's dependence

- the self's vulnerability

- the ego's potential

- the fantasy's possibility

- the mind's susceptibility

The Being is free, but not self-sustaining.

The Being Was Whole

Before the turning, the Being is:

- aligned

- open

- connected

- transparent

- integrated

- unhidden

There is no self-deception.
There is no egoic distortion.
There is no fantasy.
There is no projection.
There is no drift.

The Being is what it was made to be.

The Being Was Not Yet Divided

The heart, self, mind, and world are in harmony.

The heart is the center.
The self is the expression.
The mind is the interpreter.
The world is the environment.

There is no conflict between them.
No fracture.
No distortion.

This is the original anatomy.

The Being Was Not Yet Hidden

There is no secrecy.
No shame.
No concealment.

The heart is visible.
The self is open.
The world is safe.
The Source is near.

This is the condition before the fall.

The Being Was Not Yet Its Own Source

This is the most important truth of Movement II.

The Being did not define itself.
It did not generate its own meaning.
It did not construct its own identity.
It did not create its own truth.

The Being received everything:

- identity

- purpose

- meaning

- alignment

- life

This is the architecture that makes the fall possible.
Because the fall is not a moral failure.
It is a structural inversion.

Where This Leads

Movement II ends with the Being whole, aligned, open, and dependent on the Source.

Movement III will show the inversion:

- the self rises

- the ego awakens

- fantasy begins

- the heart hides

- the mind projects

- the world exposes

But we cannot map the collapse until we have mapped the design.

MOVEMENT III

The Anatomy of The Being
How Man Was Formed - Genesis 2

To understand what man became, we must first understand what man *is*.
Genesis 2 is the only record of the human Being in its original, undistorted architecture.
It reveals a structure that no discipline can reconstruct and no philosophy can infer without revelation.

The Being is formed as a unified three-part reality:

1. The physical body

2. The spiritual breath

3. The soul — the interior life

From these three, the full architecture of the heart, the self, the ego, the mind, and the world emerges.

This movement reveals the Being as it was designed.

The Physical Body

"Formed from the dust of the ground."

The physical body is intentional.
It is shaped, structured, and ordered.

The physical dimension includes:

- the body

- the senses

- the brain

- the nervous system

- the biological life sustained by breath and blood

The body is the vessel of the Being.
It is the outward form through which the inner life expresses itself.

But the body alone is not the human being.
It is the form, not the life.

The Spiritual Breath

"And God breathed into his nostrils the breath of life."

This breath is not oxygen.
It is not chemistry.
It is not biological animation.

It is spirit.

The spiritual breath is:

- the origin of identity

- the source of meaning

- the connection to the Source

- the foundation of the heart

- the life that animates the soul

Without this breath, man is dust.
With this breath, man becomes a living soul.

This is the spiritual dimension of the Being.

The Soul

"And man became a living soul."

The soul is the interior life that emerges when body
and spirit unite.
It is the conscious center of the human Being.

The soul includes:

Consciousness

The awareness of existence.
The recognition of self and world.

Awareness

The outward orientation.
The ability to perceive, engage, and respond.

Emotion

The capacity to feel, desire, rejoice, fear, and grieve.
Emotion is the expression of the heart's orientation.

Intellect

The ability to think, reason, imagine, and understand.
The intellect is the instrument of the soul, not its
authority.

The soul is the seat of the heart.
It is where the self emerges.
It is where the ego can awaken.
It is where fantasy can form.

The soul is the center of the Being.

The Heart

The heart is the deepest part of the soul.
It is the seat of motive, desire, orientation, and truth.

Before the fall, the heart is:

- open

- aligned

- transparent

- receptive

- unhidden

The heart is not deceitful.
The heart is not divided.
The heart is not its own source.

The heart is oriented outward toward the Source.

This is the original condition of man.

The Self

The self is the expression of the heart.
It is the outward manifestation of the interior life.

Before the fall, the self is:

- relational

- responsive

- outward-facing

- transparent

The self does not seek its own meaning.
It does not construct its own identity.
It does not turn inward.

The self interprets reality **accurately** because the heart
is aligned with the Source.

The self is the interpreter of experience.

The Ego

Before the fall, the ego is dormant.
It is not active.
It is not distorting.
It is not awakened.

The ego is the potential for self-centeredness, but not
the reality.
It is the possibility of autonomy, but not the choice.

The ego sleeps.

The Mind

The mind is not the interpreter of reality.
It is the projection surface where interpretation
appears.

The mind is:

- the screen

- the field

- the canvas

- the display

It does not:

- interpret

- choose

- decide

- judge

- distort

- create meaning

The self interprets.
The mind displays.

This is the architecture:

- The heart orients.

- The self interprets.

- The mind projects.

Before the fall, the mind is clear because the self is
aligned.

The World

The world is the environment in which the Being lives.
Before the fall, the world is not hostile.
It is not threatening.
It is not exposing.

The world is the environment of:

- order

- meaning

- purpose

- participation

The world reflects the alignment of the Being.

The Unified Being

Before the fall, the entire architecture is unified.

The body expresses the soul.
The soul responds to the spirit.
The spirit connects to the Source.
The heart is open.
The self is outward.
The ego is dormant.
The mind is clear.
The world is safe.

This is the Being as it was designed.
This is what man is.
This is the blueprint that makes the fall intelligible.

MOVEMENT IV

The Turning of The Being
How the Self Became the Center and the Heart
Became Hidden

The heart is open.
The self is outward.
The ego is aligned.
The mind is clear.
The world is safe.
The Source is near.

But Genesis 3 reveals the moment this architecture inverts.
The fall is not primarily moral.
It is structural.

The fall is the moment the Being turns inward.
This is the moment the self becomes the center.
This is the moment the ego shifts from alignment to autonomy.
This is the moment fantasy begins.
This is the moment the heart hides.

Everything that follows in human history begins here.

The Arrival of The Deception

The Deception does not attack the body.
It does not attack the intellect.
It does not attack the emotions.

It attacks the **orientation** of the heart.

The Deception introduces a new possibility:

"You can be your own source."

This is the first time the Being is invited to:

- interpret reality apart from the Source

- define truth from within

- construct meaning independently

- turn inward instead of outward

The Deception is not merely a lie.
It is a **reinterpretation of reality**.

This is the seed of the fall.

The Self Interprets Without the Source

The moment the Being entertains The Deception, the architecture shifts.

The self begins to interpret reality **without** the heart's alignment to the Source.

This is the first misinterpretation in human history.

The self interprets:

- the fruit

- the command

- the consequence

- the identity

- the Source

all through its own lens.

This is the beginning of autonomy.

The Ego Shifts From Alignment to Autonomy

Before the fall, the ego is aligned.
It is the part of the self that allows individuality, agency, and personal identity — but under the heart's orientation toward the Source.

The ego is:

- present

- integrated

- ordered

- healthy

- relational

But when the self interprets reality without the Source, the ego shifts.

It becomes:

- the distorting force

- the filter of meaning

- the defender of autonomy

- the protector of the inward turn

The ego is no longer aligned.
It becomes the guardian of the self-as-center.

This is the structural inversion.

Fantasy Begins

Fantasy is not imagination.
Fantasy is the **false interpretation** the self constructs to justify the inward turn.

Fantasy is the story the self tells itself to avoid the truth of the heart.

Fantasy is:

- the illusion of independence

- the illusion of self-sufficiency

- the illusion of hiddenness

- the illusion of control

Fantasy is the self's attempt to live without the Source.

This is the first lie the Being tells itself.

The Mind Projects the New Interpretation

The mind does not interpret.
It only displays.

Once the self interprets reality through the ego's distortion, the mind projects that interpretation as truth.

The mind becomes:

- the screen of illusion

- the field of fantasy

- the display of distortion

The mind is not broken.
It is obedient.

It shows whatever the self believes.

The Heart Hides

The first action after the turning is hiding.

The heart hides from:

- the Source

- the truth

- the other

- the self

This is the birth of the hidden heart.

The heart is no longer open.
It is no longer transparent.
It is no longer aligned.

The heart becomes:

- concealed

- protected

- inward

- divided

This is the condition Scripture later describes as
"deceitful."

The deceit is not active malice.
It is structural hiddenness.

The World Exposes the New Condition

After the turning, the world is no longer safe.
Not because the world changed, but because the Being
changed.

The world now:

- reveals the heart

- exposes the self

- confronts the ego

- disrupts fantasy

The world becomes the mirror of the interior life.

This is why the Being experiences:

- fear

- shame

- blame

- fragmentation

The world is not the problem.
The world is the exposure.

The Architecture After the Turning

The architecture is now inverted.

Before the fall:

The heart orients.
The self interprets.
The ego aligns.
The mind projects.
The world reflects.

After the fall:

The ego distorts.
The self misinterprets.
The mind displays illusion.
The world exposes the truth.

This is the human condition.

This is the anatomy of the fallen Being.

The structure every discipline tries to explain but
cannot reach.

MOVEMENT V

The Anatomy of The Fallen Being
The Hidden Heart, the Divided Self, the Autonomous
Ego, the Fantasy, the Mind, and the World

Once the Being turns inward, the entire architecture shifts.
The fall is not a moment of punishment.
It is a moment of **reconfiguration**.

The Being is still the same structure — body, spirit, soul —
but the orientation of that structure has inverted.

This movement reveals the anatomy of the fallen Being.

The Hidden Heart

The heart was once open, aligned, transparent, and receptive.
After the turning, the heart becomes hidden.

The hidden heart is:

- concealed

- protected

- inward

- divided

- unreachable by the self

The heart hides because it is no longer oriented toward the Source.
It hides because exposure now feels dangerous.
It hides because the self has become the center.

The hidden heart is the foundation of the human condition.

The Divided Self

The self was once outward-facing, relational, and transparent.
After the turning, the self becomes divided.

The divided self is:

- conflicted

- unstable

- self-protective

- self-constructing

- self-justifying

The self now interprets reality through the ego's distortion.
It no longer receives meaning; it constructs it.
It no longer expresses the heart; it protects it.

The self becomes the manager of the inward turn.

The Autonomous Ego

The ego was once aligned — the healthy structure of individuality and agency.
After the turning, the ego becomes autonomous.

The autonomous ego is:

- the defender of the self

- the filter of meaning

- the protector of fantasy

- the architect of justification

- the guardian of the inward turn

The ego's new role is to maintain the illusion that the self can be its own source.

The ego is not evil.
It is misaligned.

It is the structure that keeps the self at the center.

The Fantasy

Fantasy is the self's false interpretation of reality.
It is the story the self constructs to avoid the truth of
the heart.

Fantasy is:

- the illusion of independence

- the illusion of self-sufficiency

- the illusion of hiddenness

- the illusion of control

- the illusion of self-created meaning

Fantasy is not imagination.
It is the self's attempt to live without the Source.

Fantasy is the world the self prefers over the truth.

The Mind as Projection

The mind does not interpret.
It displays whatever the self believes.

After the turning, the mind becomes:

- the screen of illusion

- the field of fantasy

- the projection of distortion

- the display of the ego's filtered meaning

The mind is not broken.
It is obedient.

It shows the self's interpretation, not the truth.

This is why the mind cannot save the self.
It can only reveal what the self already believes.

The World as Exposure

The world was once the environment of alignment.
After the turning, the world becomes the environment
of exposure.

The world now:

- reveals the heart

- confronts the self

- disrupts fantasy

- exposes the ego

- mirrors the interior condition

The world is not the enemy.
The world is the mirror.

This is why the fallen Being experiences:

- fear

- shame

- blame

- fragmentation

- conflict

- alienation

The world exposes what the self tries to hide.

The New Architecture

After the fall, the architecture of the Being is inverted.

Before the fall:

The heart orients.
The self interprets.
The ego aligns.
The mind projects.
The world reflects.

After the fall:

The ego distorts.
The self misinterprets.
The mind displays illusion.
The world exposes the truth.
The heart hides.

This is the human condition.
This is the structure every discipline tries to explain but
cannot reach.

The anatomy of the fallen Being.

MOVEMENT VI

The Consequences of The Inverted Architecture
Drift, Fragmentation, Fantasy Cycles, Exposure, and
the Limits of Self-Repair

Once the Being turns inward, the architecture does not
simply change — it begins to **produce consequences**.
These consequences are not moral punishments.
They are structural outcomes.

The fallen architecture generates patterns that repeat
across every human life, every culture, every era, every
discipline.

This movement reveals those patterns.

Drift

Drift is the natural movement of the fallen Being away
from alignment.

Drift is:

- gradual

- subtle

- unintentional

- inevitable

Drift happens because the self is now the center, and
the self cannot sustain orientation.
The self cannot anchor itself.
The self cannot generate meaning.
The self cannot remain stable.

Drift is the slow collapse of the inward turn.

Fragmentation

Fragmentation is the internal division created by the
hidden heart and the autonomous ego.

Fragmentation appears as:

- conflicting desires

- contradictory motives

- unstable identity

- emotional volatility

- intellectual inconsistency

The Being is no longer unified.
The heart hides.
The self constructs.
The ego defends.
The mind projects.

Each part pulls in a different direction.

Fragmentation is the structural outcome of the divided self.

The Cycle of Fantasy

Fantasy is not a one-time event.
It becomes a cycle.

The cycle of fantasy follows this pattern:

1. The heart hides.

2. The self misinterprets.

3. The ego distorts.

4. The mind projects.

5. The world exposes.

6. The self constructs a new fantasy to avoid exposure.

This cycle repeats endlessly.

Fantasy is the self's attempt to maintain the illusion of autonomy.
But the world continually disrupts it.

This is why human beings live in cycles of:

- self-deception

- self-protection

- self-justification

- self-collapse

Fantasy is the architecture of the inward life.

Exposure

Exposure is the world revealing the truth the self tries to hide.

Exposure happens through:

- relationships

- conflict

- failure

- limitation

- consequence

- time

Exposure is not cruelty.
It is structural.

The world is the mirror of the heart.
It reflects what the self refuses to see.

Exposure is the collapse of fantasy.

The Limits of Self-Repair

The fallen Being cannot repair itself.

Not because it is weak.
Not because it is unworthy.
Not because it is morally corrupt.

But because the architecture is inverted.

The self cannot fix the self because:

- the self is the problem

- the ego protects the problem

- the fantasy hides the problem

- the mind projects the problem

- the world exposes the problem

- the heart cannot be reached by the self

Self-repair is structurally impossible.

This is why every human attempt at self-salvation collapses:

- self-improvement

- self-discipline

- self-reinvention

- self-definition

- self-elevation

The self cannot heal the heart it cannot access.

The Universal Human Condition

These consequences are not personal failures.
They are universal patterns.

Every human being experiences:

- drift

- fragmentation

- fantasy

- exposure

- collapse

- reconstruction

- collapse again

This is the architecture of the fallen Being.

This is the condition every discipline tries to describe.
This is the condition every human being feels.
This is the condition Scripture diagnoses.

This is the condition that makes redemption necessary.

MOVEMENT VII

The Agony of Being - *The Prison of the Inward Turn and the Dilemma to Escape*

The fallen Being does not simply suffer.
He suffers because he is **trapped inside himself**.

He feels the fracture.
He feels the drift.
He feels the dissonance.
He feels the collapse.

He feels the ache of a heart he cannot reach.
He feels the weight of a self he cannot silence.
He feels the pressure of an ego he cannot dethrone.
He feels the pull of a fantasy he cannot stop believing.

This is not emotional pain.
This is **ontological agony** — the agony of existing in
an architecture that cannot return to alignment.

This is the agony Paul names in Romans 7.
This is the agony every human being knows.

1. The Desire for Good Remains

Even after the turning, the Being still carries:

- the memory of alignment

- the longing for openness

- the ache for goodness

- the desire for truth

- the hunger for meaning

This desire is not erased by the fall.
It is intensified by it.

The fallen Being wants to do good.
He wants to choose what is right.
He wants to return to the Source.

This desire is genuine.

But desire is not ability.

2. The Ability to Do Good Is Lost

The fallen Being discovers a horrifying truth:

He cannot do the good he wants.
He does the very thing he hates.

This is not moral weakness.
This is not lack of discipline.
This is not psychological instability.

This is **structural inversion**.

Because:

- the heart is hidden

- the self is the center

- the ego distorts

- the fantasy protects

- the mind projects

- the world exposes

The architecture pulls him inward.

He wants to choose truth,
but the ego filters it.

He wants to act rightly,
but the self interprets wrongly.

He wants to escape,
but the fantasy shields him from reality.

He wants to be free,
but the mind projects illusion.

He wants to return,
but the heart cannot be reached.

This is the dilemma to escape.

3. The Being Becomes a Prisoner

The fallen Being is not imprisoned by the world.
He is imprisoned by his own architecture.

He is a prisoner of:

- his own interpretations

- his own distortions

- his own illusions

- his own protections

- his own inwardness

He is locked inside himself.

This is why Paul cries:

"I am a prisoner of the law of sin within me."

Not sin as behaviour.
Sin as **inwardness**.
Sin as **self-as-center**.
Sin as **structural captivity**.

The Being becomes a slave to his own master —
the self he cannot dethrone.

4. The More He Tries to Escape, the Deeper He Sinks

Every attempt at escape strengthens the prison.

When he tries to do good:
the ego distorts the motive.

When he tries to discipline himself:
the self becomes more central.

When he tries to understand himself:
the fantasy deepens.

When he tries to correct his mind:
the projection intensifies.

When he tries to heal himself:
the heart hides further.

The architecture resists escape.

The inward turn reinforces itself.

5. The Dilemma Is Not Psychological — It Is Ontological

The fallen Being lives in a contradiction:

- He wants the good.

- He chooses the opposite.

- He hates the opposite.

- He cannot stop choosing it.

This is not hypocrisy.
This is not weakness.
This is not confusion.

This is the **inverted architecture**.

This is the agony of being.

This is the dilemma Paul names.
This is the dilemma every human feels.

This is the dilemma the reader now recognizes in themselves.

6. The Architecture Locks Itself

After the fall, the architecture becomes a closed system:

- the heart hides

- the self interprets

- the ego distorts

- the fantasy protects

- the mind projects

- the world exposes

And the cycle repeats.

The Being cannot escape because the Being is the prison.

This is the agony of being.
This is the universal human condition.
This is the structural tragedy of existence after the turning.

MOVEMENT VIII

The Architecture of Return

Why the Way Out Cannot Come From Within

The fallen Being has reached the limit of himself.
He has discovered the agony of being —
the desire for good without the ability to do it,
the longing for escape without the power to escape,
the ache for alignment without the means to return.

He has discovered the Romans-7 dilemma:

"I want to do good, but I do what I hate."

He has discovered the prison of the inward turn.

Now he discovers something even more devastating:

There is no path back from inside the architecture.

This movement reveals why the return must come
from beyond the self.

1. The Heart Cannot Open Itself

The heart is hidden.
It cannot unhide itself.

The heart cannot:

- expose itself

- heal itself

- reorient itself

- return itself to the Source

The heart is deeper than the self.
The self cannot reach it.

This is why the return cannot begin with the heart.

2. The Self Cannot Dethrone Itself

The self is now the center.
It cannot stop being the center.

The self cannot:

- surrender itself

- silence itself

- unmake itself

- remove itself from the throne

The self cannot dethrone the self.

This is why the return cannot begin with the self.

3. The Ego Cannot Realign Itself

The ego is now the guardian of the inward turn.
It exists to protect the self-as-center.

The ego cannot:

- release control

- stop distorting

- stop filtering meaning

- stop defending autonomy

The ego cannot realign because realignment would require the ego to betray its own function.

This is why the return cannot begin with the ego.

4. Fantasy Cannot Collapse From Within

Fantasy is the self's protective illusion.
It shields the self from exposure.

Fantasy cannot:

- reveal the truth

- dismantle itself

- contradict the ego

- expose the heart

Fantasy cannot collapse from within because collapse would require the self to face the truth it is hiding from.

This is why the return cannot begin with fantasy.

5. The Mind Cannot Correct the Self

The mind is the projection surface.
It displays whatever the self believes.

The mind cannot:

- override the ego

- correct interpretation

- reveal the heart

- expose fantasy

The mind cannot correct the self because the mind is not the interpreter — it is the display.

This is why the return cannot begin with the mind.

6. The World Cannot Heal the Heart

The world exposes.
It does not restore.

The world cannot:

- reorient the heart

- realign the ego

- correct the self

- collapse fantasy

- heal the interior life

The world reveals the condition.
It cannot repair it.

This is why the return cannot begin with the world.

7. The Architecture Cannot Save Itself

The fallen architecture is a closed system:

- the heart hides

- the self interprets

- the ego distorts

- the fantasy protects

- the mind projects

- the world exposes

Every part reinforces the inward turn.
Every part protects the prison.
Every part resists return.

The architecture cannot save itself because the
architecture *is* the problem.

This is the revelation:

**The way out cannot come from within.
The return must come from beyond the self.**

This is the beginning of hope.
Not the arrival of redemption —
but the first structural possibility of it.

8. The Necessity of an External Source

If the heart cannot open itself,
and the self cannot dethrone itself,

and the ego cannot realign itself,
and the fantasy cannot collapse itself,
and the mind cannot correct itself,
and the world cannot heal the heart…

Then the return requires:

- a Source beyond the heart

- a truth beyond the self

- a power beyond the ego

- a reality beyond fantasy

- a revelation beyond the mind

- a presence beyond the world

The return requires **intervention**.
Not moral effort.
Not intellectual clarity.
Not emotional resolve.
Not behavioural change.

The return requires **a new architecture entering the old one**.

This is the threshold of redemption.

9. The First Crack of Light

Movement VIII ends not with the return itself,
but with the realization that return is possible —
not because the Being can climb out,
but because the Source can break in.

This is the first crack of light in the prison of the inward turn.

MOVEMENT IX

The Return To Sanity

The First Movement Back Toward Reality

The fallen Being has reached the end of himself.
He has discovered the agony of being —
the desire for good without the ability to do it,
the longing for escape without the power to escape,
the ache for alignment without the means to return.

He has discovered the Romans-7 dilemma:

"I want to do good, but I do what I hate."

He has discovered the prison of the inward turn.

Now he discovers something new:

Sanity is not something he creates.
Sanity is something he returns to.

Sanity is not psychological stability.
Sanity is **alignment with reality** — the original
architecture restored.

This movement reveals the first steps toward sanity.

1. Sanity Begins With Reality Entering the Prison

The fallen Being cannot escape from within.
The architecture is closed.
The heart is hidden.
The self is the center.
The ego is the guardian.
The fantasy is the shield.
The mind is the projection.
The world is the exposure.

There is no path outward.

So sanity begins with something else:

Reality enters inward.

Not the Being reaching out,
but the Source breaking in.

This is the first movement of sanity.

2. Sanity Requires an External Source

The fallen architecture cannot restore itself.

- The heart cannot open itself.

- The self cannot dethrone itself.

- The ego cannot realign itself.

- The fantasy cannot collapse itself.

- The mind cannot correct itself.

- The world cannot heal the heart.

The return to sanity requires:

- a truth beyond the self

- a presence beyond the ego

- a reality beyond fantasy

- a revelation beyond the mind

- a Source beyond the world

Sanity is not self-generated.
Sanity is **received**.

3. The Heart Is Opened From the Outside

The heart is the deepest part of the Being.
It is hidden, protected, unreachable.

The self cannot reach it.
The ego cannot touch it.

The mind cannot access it.
The world cannot penetrate it.

So the return to sanity begins here:

The heart is opened from the outside.

Not by force.
Not by effort.
Not by discipline.

But by presence.

The heart opens when reality enters.

4. The Self Is Dethroned by Something Greater

The self cannot stop being the center.
It cannot surrender itself.
It cannot unmake itself.

So the return to sanity requires:

a greater center.

Something so real, so weighty, so true
that the self cannot remain on the throne.

The self is dethroned not by effort,
but by encounter.

Sanity begins when the self is displaced
by something more real than itself.

5. The Ego Is Realigned Under a New Orientation

The ego is the guardian of the inward turn.
It protects the self-as-center.
It filters meaning.
It distorts truth.

The ego cannot realign itself.

But when the heart opens
and the self is dethroned,
the ego is no longer the highest authority.

It is no longer the protector of autonomy.
It is no longer the interpreter of meaning.

The ego becomes aligned again —
not erased,
but ordered.

This is the first taste of sanity.

6. Fantasy Collapses in the Presence of Truth

Fantasy cannot collapse from within.
It collapses when reality enters.

When the heart opens,
and the self is dethroned,
and the ego is realigned…

Fantasy loses its power.

The illusions that once protected the inward turn
cannot survive the presence of truth.

Fantasy dissolves
not by effort,
but by exposure to reality.

This is sanity returning.

7. The Mind Projects a New Interpretation

The mind does not interpret.
It displays.

Once the self is dethroned
and the ego realigned
and fantasy collapsed…

The mind becomes clear.

It projects:

- truth instead of distortion

- reality instead of illusion

- alignment instead of inwardness

The mind becomes the canvas of sanity.

8. The World Is Reinterpreted Through Alignment

The world no longer exposes the inward turn.
It reflects the new orientation.

The world becomes:

- meaningful

- coherent

- ordered

- participatory

The world is no longer the mirror of the hidden heart.
It becomes the environment of the restored heart.

This is the return to sanity.

9. Sanity Is the Return to Being

Sanity is not improvement.
Sanity is not discipline.
Sanity is not self-control.

Sanity is:

- the heart opened

- the self dethroned

- the ego realigned

- the fantasy collapsed

- the mind clarified

- the world reinterpreted

- the Source restored as center

Sanity is the return to the architecture.

Sanity is the return to reality.
Sanity is the return to alignment.
Sanity is the return to being.

MOVEMENT X

The Heart That Hungers For Truth

How the Heart Awakens, Hears, and Receives Reality

The return to sanity begins with the heart.
Not the mind.
Not the will.
Not the behaviour.

The heart is the deepest part of the Being.
It is the seat of orientation.
It is the place where truth is recognized, received, and
responded to.

The fall hid the heart.
Restoration begins when the heart hungers again.

1. The Heart That Hungers for Truth

Even in its hiddenness,
even in its inwardness,
even in its fragmentation…

The heart still hungers.

It hungers for:

- reality

- clarity

- meaning

- alignment

- truth

This hunger is not emotional.
It is **ontological memory** —
the echo of Eden still beating inside the fallen
architecture.

The heart hungers because it was made for truth.
It hungers because it remembers truth.
It hungers because it cannot live without truth.

This hunger is the first sign of restoration.

2. The Heart That Hears the Truth

The heart does not open itself.
It responds.

When truth approaches,
the heart recognizes it.

Not intellectually.
Not analytically.
Not philosophically.

But **instinctively**.

The heart hears truth the way the ear hears sound,
the way the eye sees light,
the way the lungs receive air.

Truth is the heart's native language.

When truth speaks,
the heart awakens.

When truth calls,
the heart stirs.

When truth draws near,
the heart listens.

This is the second movement of restoration.

3. The Truth That Enters the Heart

Truth does not remain outside.
Truth enters.

Not as information.
Not as doctrine.
Not as concept.

Truth enters as **presence**.

Truth enters as **reality**.

Truth enters as **alignment**.

When truth enters the heart:

- the inward turn loosens

- the hiddenness cracks

- the fear softens

- the ego trembles

- the self loses its throne

- the fantasy begins to dissolve

Truth does not argue with the heart.
Truth **reorders** the heart.

This is the third movement of restoration.

4. The Heart Turns Toward the Source

When truth enters,
the heart turns.

This turning is not effort.
It is response.

The heart turns toward:

- the Source

- the real

- the true

- the good

- the beautiful

This turning is the reversal of the fall.
This turning is the beginning of alignment.
This turning is the return to sanity.

The heart turns because truth has entered.

5. The Heart Becomes the New Center of the Being

Once the heart turns,
the entire architecture begins to shift.

- The self is dethroned.

- The ego realigns.

- Fantasy collapses.

- The mind becomes clear.

- The world becomes coherent.

The heart becomes the new center —
not as ruler,
but as orientation.

This is the restoration of the original design.

6. Truth Does What the Being Cannot Do

The fallen Being cannot:

- open the heart

- dethrone the self

- realign the ego

- collapse fantasy

- clarify the mind

- reinterpret the world

But truth can.

Truth enters the heart.
Truth reorders the architecture.
Truth restores the Being.

Truth does what the Being cannot do.

This is the miracle of restoration.

7. The Heart That Hungers, Hears, and Receives

Restoration is not improvement.
Restoration is not discipline.
Restoration is not self-control.

Restoration is:

- the heart hungering

- the heart hearing

- the heart receiving

- the heart turning

- the heart reorienting

- the heart restoring the architecture

Restoration begins **in** the heart
because the heart is the place where truth enters.

restored heart begins to reshape identity, meaning,
purpose, and the entire lived experience of the Being

MOVEMENT X

When Truth Enters The Heart

The Act of the Spirit, the Acceptance of Alignment, and the Beginning of Restoration

The fallen Being cannot restore himself.
He cannot open his heart.
He cannot dethrone his self.
He cannot realign his ego.
He cannot collapse his fantasy.
He cannot clarify his mind.
He cannot reconcile with the world.

Man cannot do these things without redemption.

Redemption begins at one point only:

When Truth enters the heart.

This is the act of the Spirit.
This is the moment of alignment.
This is the beginning of restoration.

1. The Heart Hungers for Truth — But Cannot Reach It

Even in its hiddenness, the heart hungers.

It hungers for:

- reality

- clarity

- meaning

- goodness

- alignment

But hunger is not access.
Desire is not ability.

The heart longs for Truth,
but cannot open itself to Truth.

This is the tragedy of the fall.
This is why redemption is necessary.

2. Truth Approaches the Heart

Truth does not wait for the heart to open.
Truth **comes to the heart**.

Truth approaches:

- gently

- steadily

- faithfully

- personally

Truth does not demand entry.
Truth **offers alignment**.

This is the first act of the Spirit —
Truth drawing near.

3. The Heart Hears the Truth

The heart recognizes Truth.
Not intellectually.
Not philosophically.
Not emotionally.

But **ontologically**.

The heart hears Truth the way:

- the ear hears sound

- the eye sees light

- the lungs receive breath

Truth is the heart's native environment.

This hearing is the second act of the Spirit —
Truth awakening the heart.

4. The Heart Accepts the Offer of Alignment

Truth does not force its way in.
Truth offers alignment.

The heart responds.

The heart says:

"Yes."

This "yes" is not willpower.
It is not discipline.
It is not moral effort.

It is **surrender** —
the heart accepting what it cannot create.

This is the third act of the Spirit —
the heart receiving Truth.

5. Truth Enters the Heart

This is the moment everything changes.

Truth enters:

- not as information

- not as doctrine

- not as concept

Truth enters as **presence**.
Truth enters as **life**.
Truth enters as **alignment**.

When Truth enters the heart:

- the inward turn loosens

- the hiddenness cracks

- the fear softens

- the ego trembles

- the self loses its throne

- the fantasy begins to dissolve

This is the fourth act of the Spirit —
Truth inhabiting the heart.

6. Restoration Begins From the Inside Out

Once Truth enters the heart:

- the self is dethroned

- the ego realigns

- fantasy collapses

- the mind becomes clear

- the world becomes coherent

Restoration is not self-improvement.
Restoration is **Truth reordering the architecture**.

This is the fifth act of the Spirit —
the re-creation of the Being.

7. The World Becomes the Reflection of the New Heart

The fallen world exposed the inward turn.
The restored world reflects the new orientation.

The world becomes:

- meaningful

- relational

- participatory

- coherent

The world is no longer the mirror of the hidden heart.
It becomes the environment of the restored heart.

This is the sixth act of the Spirit —
the reconciliation of the world.

8. Redemption Is the Beginning of Restoration

Redemption is not the end.
It is the beginning.

Redemption is:

- Truth entering the heart

- the heart accepting alignment

- the Spirit reordering the architecture

- the Being turning outward again

- the world becoming reconciled

Redemption is the moment the impossible becomes possible.
Redemption is the moment the architecture begins to heal.
Redemption is the moment the Being returns to Being.

MOVEMENT XI

The New Orientation

How the Redeemed Heart Reorders the Being and Rewrites Reality

When Truth enters the heart, the architecture begins to
turn.
Not by effort.
Not by discipline.
Not by self-reform.

But by **redemption**.

The heart has accepted the offer of alignment.
The Spirit has entered.
Truth has taken its place at the center.

Now the Being begins to live from a new orientation.

1. The Heart Becomes the New Center of the Being

Before redemption, the heart was hidden.
Now the heart is open.

Before redemption, the heart was unreachable.
Now Truth dwells within it.

Before redemption, the heart was silent.
Now the heart speaks.

The heart becomes:

- the compass

- the orientation point

- the seat of alignment

- the place where Truth lives

The heart is no longer the prisoner of the self.
The heart becomes the center of the Being again.

This is the first sign of the new orientation.

2. The Self Moves Out of the Center

The self was once the ruler.
The self was once the interpreter.
The self was once the architect of meaning.

But when Truth enters the heart,
the self is dethroned.

Not destroyed.
Not erased.
Not humiliated.

Relocated.

The self becomes:

- responsive instead of controlling

- receptive instead of defensive

- relational instead of isolated

- aligned instead of autonomous

The self is no longer the master.
It becomes the servant of Truth.

This is the second sign of the new orientation.

3. The Ego Realigns Under the Heart

The ego once guarded the inward turn.
It protected the self-as-center.
It filtered meaning.
It distorted truth.

But when Truth enters the heart,
the ego loses its old assignment.

The ego becomes:

- ordered

- integrated

- healthy

- relational

- grounded

The ego is no longer the enforcer of autonomy.
It becomes the structure that enables individuality
without isolation.

This is the third sign of the new orientation.

4. Fantasy Collapses Under the Weight of Truth

Fantasy once shielded the self from exposure.
It created illusions to protect the inward turn.

But when Truth enters the heart,
fantasy cannot survive.

Fantasy collapses because:

- the heart no longer hides

- the self no longer fears exposure

- the ego no longer distorts

- the mind no longer projects illusion

Fantasy dissolves not by effort,
but by irrelevance.

This is the fourth sign of the new orientation.

5. The Mind Becomes Clear and Honest

The mind once displayed illusion.
Now it displays Truth.

The mind becomes:

- clear

- coherent

- grounded

- aligned

The mind no longer invents meaning.
It receives meaning.

The mind no longer projects fantasy.
It reflects reality.

This is the fifth sign of the new orientation.

6. The World Is Seen Through the Restored Heart

The fallen Being saw the world as threat.
The redeemed Being sees the world as revelation.

The world becomes:

- meaningful

- relational

- participatory

- coherent

The world is no longer the mirror of the hidden heart.
It becomes the environment of the restored heart.

This is the sixth sign of the new orientation.

7. Identity Is Rewritten From the Inside Out

Identity was once constructed by the self.
Now identity is received from Truth.

Identity becomes:

- stable

- grounded

- relational

- aligned

Identity is no longer a story the self tells itself.
Identity is the reality the heart receives.

This is the seventh sign of the new orientation.

8. Meaning Returns to the Being

Meaning was once fantasy.
Now meaning is revelation.

Meaning becomes:

- coherent

- grounded

- true

- relational

Meaning is no longer self-constructed.
Meaning is received from the Source.

This is the eighth sign of the new orientation.

9. The Being Lives From the Heart Outward

The fallen Being lived from the self inward.
The redeemed Being lives from the heart outward.

The architecture becomes:

heart → self → ego → mind → world

This is the original design.
This is the redeemed design.
This is the new orientation.

The Being is no longer trapped inside himself.
He is aligned with Truth again.

He is aligned with reality again.
He is aligned with the Source again.

He has returned to Being.

MOVEMENT XII

What It Means To Be Human

The Human Being as the Creature Who Receives, Reflects, and Reveals Truth

When Truth enters the heart, the architecture turns.
When the architecture turns, the Being is restored.
When the Being is restored, the world is reconciled.

But beneath all of this lies a deeper revelation:

This is what it means to be human.

Humanity is not defined by intelligence.
Not by consciousness.
Not by morality.
Not by creativity.

Humanity is defined by **receptivity** —
the capacity to receive Truth,
to be transformed by Truth,
and to reflect Truth into the world.

This movement reveals the redeemed human.

1. The Human Being Is the Creature Who Can Receive Truth

No other creature has this capacity.

- Animals respond to instinct.

- Angels respond to command.

- Nature responds to order.

- Machines respond to input.

Only the human heart responds to **Truth**.

Only the human heart:

- hungers for Truth

- hears Truth

- recognizes Truth

- receives Truth

- is transformed by Truth

This is the essence of humanity.

Humanity is the creature whose heart can be entered by Truth.

2. The Human Being Is the Creature Who Can Be Redeemed

Redemption is not a moral category.
It is an ontological one.

Only the human being:

- can fall

- can hunger

- can hear

- can surrender

- can receive

- can be restored

This is what makes humanity unique.

Humanity is not the creature who sins.
Humanity is the creature who can be **saved**.

This is what it means to be human.

3. The Human Being Is the Creature Whose Heart Can Turn

When Truth enters the heart,
the heart turns toward the Source.

This turning is not:

- willpower

- discipline

- moral effort

It is **response**.

The human being is the creature whose heart can turn

—

from inwardness to openness,
from fantasy to reality,
from self to Source.

This turning is the essence of humanity.

4. The Human Being Is the Creature Who Can Be Recreated

When Truth enters the heart,
the Spirit begins the work of re-creation.

This is not improvement.
This is not self-help.
This is not moral reform.

This is **new creation**.

The human being is the creature who can be:

- re-aligned

- re-ordered

- re-centered

- re-made

This is what it means to be human.

5. The Human Being Is the Creature Who Reflects What It Receives

The fallen human reflects fantasy.
The redeemed human reflects Truth.

The human being is the creature who:

- mirrors the heart

- expresses the center

- reveals the orientation

- embodies the alignment

If the heart receives illusion,
the world becomes illusion.

If the heart receives Truth,
the world becomes revelation.

This is the human condition.

6. The Human Being Is the Creature Who Participates in Reality

The fallen human survives the world.
The redeemed human participates in it.

The human being is the creature who:

- engages

- responds

- relates

- creates

- reveals

The human being is not a spectator of reality.
The human being is a participant in reality.

This is what it means to be human.

7. The Human Being Is the Creature Who Reveals the Source

When Truth enters the heart,
the human being becomes a window.

A window through which:

- alignment is seen

- reality is revealed

- meaning is expressed

- the Source is known

The human being is the creature who reveals the One who entered the heart.

This is the destiny of humanity.

8. Humanity Is Not the Problem — Humanity Is the Design

The fall distorted humanity.
Redemption restores humanity.

Humanity is not the obstacle.
Humanity is the vessel.

Humanity is not the failure.
Humanity is the possibility.

Humanity is not the tragedy.
Humanity is the calling.

To be human is to be the creature who can receive Truth
and reveal Truth to the world.

This is what it means to be human.

MOVEMENT XIII

The Restoration of Relationship

What It Means to Be Human in the World After Truth Enters the Heart

Redemption is not the end of the story.
It is the beginning of humanity.

When Truth enters the heart,
the Being is restored.
When the Being is restored,
the world becomes different.
When the world becomes different,
relationship becomes possible again.

This movement reveals what it means to be human **in
the world** after alignment.

1. The Restored Heart Turns Toward Others

The fallen heart turned inward.
The redeemed heart turns outward.

The restored heart:

- sees others

- hears others

- recognizes others

- responds to others

The heart no longer hides.
The heart no longer protects itself.
The heart no longer interprets others through fear.

The heart becomes relational again.

This is the first sign of restored humanity.

2. The Self Becomes Capable of Love

Before redemption, the self could only:

- protect

- defend

- interpret

- control

- withdraw

After Truth enters the heart,
the self becomes capable of love.

Not sentimental love.
Not emotional affection.
Not moral obligation.

But **ontological love** —
the self giving what it has received.

The self becomes:

- generous

- open

- present

- responsive

The self no longer demands.
The self gives.

This is the second sign of restored humanity.

3. The Ego Becomes a Bridge, Not a Barrier

The fallen ego separated the Being from others.
The redeemed ego connects the Being to others.

The ego becomes:

- a boundary that enables intimacy

- a structure that supports individuality

- a bridge that allows relationship

- a vessel that carries presence

The ego no longer distorts others.
It allows others to be seen as they are.

This is the third sign of restored humanity.

4. Fantasy No Longer Shapes Relationship

Fantasy once shaped every interaction:

- projection

- assumption

- fear

- illusion

- misinterpretation

But when Truth enters the heart,
fantasy collapses.

Relationship becomes grounded in:

- reality

- clarity

- truth

- presence

The Being no longer relates to others through illusion.
He relates to others through Truth.

This is the fourth sign of restored humanity.

5. The Mind Sees Others Clearly

The mind once projected its own wounds onto others.
Now the mind reflects Truth.

The mind sees:

- the dignity of others

- the complexity of others

- the wounds of others

- the beauty of others

- the humanity of others

The mind becomes the instrument of compassion.

This is the fifth sign of restored humanity.

6. The World Becomes a Place of Relationship

The fallen Being survived the world.
The redeemed Being participates in it.

The world becomes:

- a field of connection

- a space of meaning

- a context for love

- a place of belonging

The world is no longer the enemy.
The world becomes the environment of relationship.

This is the sixth sign of restored humanity.

7. Humanity Becomes a Mirror of the Source

When Truth enters the heart,
the human being becomes a mirror.

A mirror that reflects:

- alignment

- goodness

- clarity

- reality

- love

The human being becomes the creature who reveals
the Source
through relationship.

This is the seventh sign of restored humanity.

8. Relationship Becomes the Expression of Redemption

Redemption is not private.
Redemption is relational.

The restored heart:

- reconciles

- forgives

- listens

- understands

- embraces

- participates

Relationship becomes the outward expression
of the inward restoration.

This is what it means to be human in the world.

9. Humanity Is Fulfilled in Relationship

The fallen Being was alone.
The redeemed Being is connected.

Humanity is fulfilled when:

- the heart is open

- the self is aligned

- the ego is ordered

- the mind is clear

- the world is reconciled

- relationship is restored

This is the fullness of humanity.
This is the purpose of humanity.
This is the destiny of humanity.

To be human is to be the creature
who receives Truth
and reveals Truth
through relationship.

MOVEMENT XIV

The Human Vocation

The Calling of the Redeemed Human in a Reconciled World

When Truth enters the heart, the Being is restored.
When the Being is restored, relationship is healed.
When relationship is healed, the world becomes reconciled.

But restoration is not the end.
It is the beginning of **vocation**.

The redeemed human is not merely aligned.
The redeemed human is **sent**.

This movement reveals the purpose of the human being after redemption.

1. The Human Being Is Called to Reveal Truth

The redeemed human is not the source of Truth.
The redeemed human is the **vessel** of Truth.

The human vocation begins here:

To reveal what the heart has received.

The redeemed human becomes:

- a window

- a mirror

- a witness

- a presence

The human being reveals the Source
by embodying the alignment of the heart.

This is the first dimension of vocation.

2. The Human Being Is Called to Love

Love is not sentiment.
Love is not emotion.
Love is not affection.

Love is **alignment expressed relationally**.

The redeemed human loves because:

- the heart is open

- the self is dethroned

- the ego is ordered

- the mind is clear

- the world is reconciled

Love becomes the natural expression
of the restored architecture.

This is the second dimension of vocation.

3. The Human Being Is Called to Participate in Reality

The fallen human survived the world.
The redeemed human participates in it.

Participation means:

- engaging

- responding

- creating

- cultivating

- stewarding

The redeemed human does not escape the world.
He enters it more deeply.

This is the third dimension of vocation.

4. The Human Being Is Called to Heal What Was Broken

The redeemed heart becomes a healing presence.

Not by force.
Not by strategy.
Not by superiority.

But by **alignment**.

Where the redeemed human stands:

- clarity enters confusion

- truth enters illusion

- presence enters isolation

- love enters fear

- meaning enters fragmentation

The human being becomes a point of restoration
in the world.

This is the fourth dimension of vocation.

5. The Human Being Is Called to Carry Meaning

Meaning is no longer self-constructed.
Meaning is received.

The redeemed human carries meaning into:

- work

- relationship

- community

- creation

- culture

Meaning becomes the atmosphere around the redeemed human.

This is the fifth dimension of vocation.

6. The Human Being Is Called to Embody Alignment

The redeemed human does not preach alignment.
He **embodies** it.

Alignment becomes visible in:

- presence

- posture

- speech

- action

- relationship

- vocation

The redeemed human becomes a living architecture of Truth.

This is the sixth dimension of vocation.

7. The Human Being Is Called to Reflect the Source

The redeemed human is not the Source.
But the redeemed human reflects the Source.

Reflection is not performance.
Reflection is not imitation.
Reflection is not effort.

Reflection is **being**.

When the heart is aligned,
the Being reflects the One who aligned it.

This is the seventh dimension of vocation.

8. The Human Being Is Called to Live Fully Human

The fallen human was less than human.
The redeemed human becomes fully human.

To be fully human is to:

- receive Truth

- reflect Truth

- reveal Truth

- participate in reality

- embody alignment

- love without fear

- live without illusion

Humanity is not the problem.
Humanity is the design.

This is the eighth dimension of vocation.

9. The Human Vocation Is the Human Destiny

The human being was created:

- to receive

- to respond

- to reflect

- to reveal

Redemption restores this destiny.

The human vocation is not a task.
It is a way of being.

The redeemed human becomes:

- the creature who receives Truth

- the creature who reflects Truth

- the creature who reveals Truth

- the creature who participates in reality

- the creature who embodies alignment

This is the purpose of humanity.
This is the destiny of humanity.
This is the vocation of humanity.

This is what it means to be human.

MOVEMENT XV

The Human Future

The Unfolding of Alignment Across Lives, Generations, and Creation

When Truth enters the heart, the Being is restored.
When the Being is restored, relationship is healed.
When relationship is healed, vocation emerges.
When vocation emerges, the world begins to change.

But the story does not end with one human heart.
Redemption is personal,
but its consequences are **cosmic**.

This movement reveals the long arc of redeemed
humanity —
the future that begins the moment Truth enters the
heart.

1. The Redeemed Human Becomes a Living Future

The redeemed human is not simply healed.
He becomes a **future in motion**.

A future where:

- alignment spreads

- clarity multiplies

- truth becomes visible

- love becomes possible

- meaning becomes shared

The redeemed human is the beginning of a new
humanity.

This is the first sign of the human future.

2. Alignment Becomes Contagious

Alignment is not private.
Alignment radiates.

Where the redeemed human stands:

- confusion begins to clear

- fear begins to soften

- illusion begins to weaken

- fragmentation begins to heal

Alignment spreads not by force,
but by presence.

This is the second sign of the human future.

3. Relationship Becomes the Architecture of Renewal

The fallen world was built on:

- fear

- projection

- self-protection

- illusion

- inwardness

The redeemed world is built on:

- openness

- truth

- presence

- love

- alignment

Every restored relationship becomes a new structure in the world.

This is the third sign of the human future.

4. Communities Form Around Truth

When one heart receives Truth,
a life changes.

When many hearts receive Truth,
a community forms.

A community shaped by:

- clarity

- humility

- generosity

- participation

- meaning

These communities become the seeds of a new world.

This is the fourth sign of the human future.

5. Generations Are Transformed by Alignment

The fallen architecture passed its distortion forward.
The redeemed architecture passes alignment forward.

Children raised by aligned hearts:

- inherit clarity

- inherit openness

- inherit truth

- inherit meaning

- inherit love

The future becomes different
because the architecture is different.

This is the fifth sign of the human future.

6. Culture Begins to Reflect the Restored Heart

Culture is the overflow of the human heart.

When the heart is fallen,
culture becomes:

- fragmented

- fearful

- self-centered

- illusion-driven

When the heart is redeemed,
culture becomes:

- coherent

- relational

- meaningful

- truthful

Art changes.
Language changes.
Institutions change.
Values change.

This is the sixth sign of the human future.

7. Creation Responds to Alignment

The world was not designed to reflect the fallen heart.
It was designed to reflect the aligned heart.

When humanity is restored:

- creation becomes coherent

- creation becomes relational

- creation becomes meaningful

- creation becomes alive

The world responds to the heart that inhabits it.

This is the seventh sign of the human future.

8. Humanity Moves Toward Its Destiny

The destiny of humanity is not:

- power

- progress

- knowledge

- achievement

The destiny of humanity is:

- alignment

- participation

- reflection

- revelation

Humanity becomes the creature who reveals the Source through the architecture of redeemed being.

This is the eighth sign of the human future.

9. The Future Begins in the Heart

The future of humanity does not begin:

- in politics

- in technology

- in culture

- in institutions

The future begins in the heart.

When Truth enters the heart:

- the Being is restored

- relationship is healed

- vocation emerges

- community forms

- culture shifts

- creation responds

- humanity moves toward destiny

The future begins the moment the heart says "yes."

This is the human future.
This is the future of the world.
This is the future of being.

MOVEMENT XV

The Human Future

The Unfolding of Alignment Across Lives, Generations, and Creation

When Truth enters the heart, the Being is restored.
When the Being is restored, relationship is healed.
When relationship is healed, vocation emerges.
When vocation emerges, the world begins to change.

But the story does not end with one human heart.
Redemption is personal,
but its consequences are **cosmic**.

This movement reveals the long arc of redeemed
humanity —
the future that begins the moment Truth enters the
heart.

1. The Redeemed Human Becomes a Living Future

The redeemed human is not simply healed.
He becomes a **future in motion**.

A future where:

- alignment spreads

- clarity multiplies

- truth becomes visible

- love becomes possible

- meaning becomes shared

The redeemed human is the beginning of a new
humanity.

This is the first sign of the human future.

2. Alignment Becomes Contagious

Alignment is not private.
Alignment radiates.

Where the redeemed human stands:

- confusion begins to clear

- fear begins to soften

- illusion begins to weaken

- fragmentation begins to heal

Alignment spreads not by force,
but by presence.

This is the second sign of the human future.

3. Relationship Becomes the Architecture of Renewal

The fallen world was built on:

- fear

- projection

- self-protection

- illusion

- inwardness

The redeemed world is built on:

- openness

- truth

- presence

- love

- alignment

Every restored relationship becomes a new structure in
the world.

This is the third sign of the human future.

4. Communities Form Around Truth

When one heart receives Truth,
a life changes.

When many hearts receive Truth,
a community forms.

A community shaped by:

- clarity

- humility

- generosity

- participation

- meaning

These communities become the seeds of a new world.

This is the fourth sign of the human future.

5. Generations Are Transformed by Alignment

The fallen architecture passed its distortion forward.
The redeemed architecture passes alignment forward.

Children raised by aligned hearts:

- inherit clarity

- inherit openness

- inherit truth

- inherit meaning

- inherit love

The future becomes different
because the architecture is different.

This is the fifth sign of the human future.

6. Culture Begins to Reflect the Restored Heart

Culture is the overflow of the human heart.

When the heart is fallen,
culture becomes:

- fragmented

- fearful

- self-centered

- illusion-driven

When the heart is redeemed,
culture becomes:

- coherent

- relational

- meaningful

- truthful

Art changes.
Language changes.
Institutions change.
Values change.

This is the sixth sign of the human future.

7. Creation Responds to Alignment

The world was not designed to reflect the fallen heart.
It was designed to reflect the aligned heart.

When humanity is restored:

- creation becomes coherent

- creation becomes relational

- creation becomes meaningful

- creation becomes alive

The world responds to the heart that inhabits it.

This is the seventh sign of the human future.

8. Humanity Moves Toward Its Destiny

The destiny of humanity is not:

- power

- progress

- knowledge

- achievement

The destiny of humanity is:

- alignment

- participation

- reflection

- revelation

Humanity becomes the creature who reveals the Source through the architecture of redeemed being.

This is the eighth sign of the human future.

9. The Future Begins in the Heart

The future of humanity does not begin:

- in politics

- in technology

- in culture

- in institutions

The future begins in the heart.

When Truth enters the heart:

- the Being is restored

- relationship is healed

- vocation emerges

- community forms

- culture shifts

- creation responds

- humanity moves toward destiny

The future begins the moment the heart says "yes."

MOVEMENT XVII

The Return To Being

The Story Completed, the Architecture Restored, the Human Revealed

The story began in Genesis 2 —
with openness, alignment, clarity, and communion.

It descended into Genesis 3 —
with inwardness, fragmentation, illusion, and fear.

It passed through:

- the agony of being

- the impossibility of escape

- the hunger for Truth

- the entrance of Truth

- the restoration of the heart

- the new orientation

- the reconciliation of the world

- the human vocation

- the human future

- the final alignment

Now the story returns to its origin —
but not as repetition.

As **restoration**.

1. The Architecture Returns to Its Original Design

The architecture is whole again:

- the heart aligned

- the self dethroned

- the ego ordered

- the mind clear

- the world reconciled

This is the architecture of Genesis 2 — restored, redeemed, fulfilled.

Being has returned to Being.

2. Humanity Returns to Its True Identity

Humanity is no longer:

- the fallen creature

- the inward creature

- the fragmented creature

Humanity becomes:

- the receptive creature

- the relational creature

- the reflective creature

- the aligned creature

Humanity becomes what it was always meant to be:

**the creature who receives Truth
and reveals Truth to the world.**

3. The Heart Returns to Openness

The heart is no longer hidden.
The heart is no longer afraid.
The heart is no longer fragmented.

The heart is:

- open

- whole

- oriented

- alive

The heart becomes the dwelling place of Truth.

This is the return to Being.

4. The Self Returns to Freedom

The self is no longer the center.
The self is no longer the architect of meaning.
The self is no longer the prisoner of illusion.

The self becomes:

- free

- grounded

- relational

- responsive

The self is restored to its true place —
not as ruler, but as steward.

This is the return to Being.

5. The Ego Returns to Order

The ego is no longer the guardian of inwardness.
It is no longer the filter of distortion.
It is no longer the architect of illusion.

The ego becomes:

- integrated

- healthy

- transparent

- relational

The ego protects the self *for* Truth,
not *from* Truth.

This is the return to Being.

6. The Mind Returns to Clarity

The mind no longer projects fantasy.
The mind no longer distorts reality.
The mind no longer interprets through fear.

The mind becomes:

- clear

- coherent

- truthful

- aligned

The mind displays what the heart receives.

This is the return to Being.

7. The World Returns to Meaning

The world is no longer the mirror of the hidden heart.
The world is no longer the field of exposure.
The world is no longer the environment of fear.

The world becomes:

- relational

- participatory

- meaningful

- alive

The world reflects the alignment of the heart.

This is the return to Being.

8. Humanity Returns to Its Vocation

Humanity becomes:

- the creature who receives

- the creature who reflects

- the creature who reveals

- the creature who participates

- the creature who loves

Humanity becomes the living architecture
through which Truth enters the world.

This is the return to Being.

9. The Story Returns to Its Beginning — Fulfilled

The story began with:

- openness

- alignment

- communion

It fell into:

- inwardness

- fragmentation

- illusion

It passed through:

- agony

- hunger

- redemption

- restoration

- vocation

- destiny

And now it returns to:

- alignment

- clarity

- communion

But now the return is deeper, fuller, truer.

The story ends where it began —
but now the heart is aligned,
the self is restored,
the world is reconciled,
and humanity is fulfilled.

This is the return to Being.
This is the completion of the architecture.
This is the restoration of the human.
This is the reconciliation of the world.
This is the destiny of creation.

This is the end of the story —
and the beginning of the true one.

MOVEMENT XVIII

The Threshold of Choice

Remain or Move Forward

You have now witnessed the entire architecture.

You have seen:

- the foundation of Being

- the inward turn

- the collapse of the self

- the agony of being

- the impossibility of escape

- the hunger for Truth

- the entrance of Truth

- the restoration of the heart

- the new orientation

- the reconciliation of the world

- the human vocation

- the human future

- the final alignment

You have seen the true foundation
and every false foundation beside it.

You have seen what it means to be human
and what it means to be redeemed.

You have seen the architecture of reality
and the architecture of illusion.

You have seen the inward turn
and the return to Being.

Now the book can go no further.
Because the next movement is not written by the

author.

It is written by **you**.

1. You Stand at the Threshold

Every human being reaches this moment.

The moment where:

- Truth has been revealed

- illusion has been exposed

- the heart has been awakened

- the architecture has been understood

And now the Being must choose.

This is the threshold.

2. You Have Seen the True Foundation

You have seen:

- the foundation that aligns with reality

- the foundation that restores the heart

- the foundation that dethrones the self

- the foundation that orders the ego

- the foundation that clarifies the mind

- the foundation that reconciles the world

- the foundation that fulfills humanity

You have seen the foundation of Being.

You have also seen the collapse of every other foundation:

- science as foundation

- self as foundation

- reason as foundation

- desire as foundation

- culture as foundation

- autonomy as foundation

You have seen their limits.
You have seen their fractures.
You have seen their consequences.

Now you know.

3. What You Do With This Knowledge Is Yours Alone

The book cannot choose for you.
The author cannot choose for you.
No philosophy can choose for you.
No argument can choose for you.

Only the heart can choose.

You must decide:

To remain
or
to move forward.

Remain in the old orientation
or move forward into alignment.

Remain in the inward turn
or move forward into Truth.

Remain in the architecture of illusion
or move forward into the architecture of Being.

Remain as you were
or become who you were made to be.

4. Every Human Being Must Make This Choice

This is the dignity of humanity:

- the heart can receive Truth

- the heart can reject Truth

- the heart can remain closed

- the heart can open

- the heart can turn

- the heart can refuse

This is the weight of being human.

This is the responsibility of being human.

This is the freedom of being human.

5. The Book Ends Here — But You Do Not

The book has taken you as far as it can.

It has shown you:

- the foundation

- the architecture

- the fall

- the agony

- the redemption

- the restoration

- the vocation

- the destiny

But the final movement is not written in ink.
It is written in your heart.

The book ends.
Your story does not.

'Free will

or

Pre-destination"

Acknowledgments

This book was not written alone.

It was shaped through conversation, refinement, and
the long discipline of listening.

To those who walked with me, challenged me, and held
space for clarity to emerge — thank you.

Your presence is woven into these pages.

To the readers who arrive at this threshold:

may the Truth that calls you also guide you.

About The Author

Conde Cagalitan is a philosopher-author and mythic architect whose work explores the structure of the human condition, the nature of alignment, and the return to Being.

He is the founder of Bridge & Beacon Publishing, where his canon continues to unfold.

He writes for those who hunger for clarity, meaning, and the restoration of the human heart.

Invitation Page

If this book has awakened something in you — a hunger, a question, a turning —

you are invited to continue the journey.

The next movement is not written here.

It is written in your life.

The Canon of Being

The Anatomy of Being is the foundational volume in a growing canon exploring:

- the structure of the human heart

- the architecture of alignment

- the restoration of humanity

- the reconciliation of the world

Future volumes will continue this work.